meditation
paths to tranquillity

This book looks at some of the principal meditation techniques used in Britain today (Transcendental, Buddhist, Baghwan Rajneesh's Dynamic, the more devotional practices of Baba Muktananda, as well as those within the Christian tradition).

Although meditation has long been associated with religious practices, you do not need to be religiously minded to benefit from it, nor do you necessarily have to change your normal way of life. Meditation is valuable to many people, and it is a very effective way of leading both the body and the mind into a state of peace and quiet. This book explores the way in which the various meditation techniques work and what they could do for you.

Published to accompany the BBC Radio series *Meditation*
First broadcast on Radio 3 from July 1978
Produced by Susan Paton

*Acknowledgment is due to the following for permission
to reproduce photographs:*

KALPTARU RAJNEESH MEDITATION CENTRE page 31
MANJUSHRI INSTITUTE FOR WISDOM CULTURE page 44
POPPERFOTO page 19
SIDDHA YOGA DHAM LONDON page 53
SPECTRUM COLOUR LIBRARY cover

Published to accompany a series of programmes prepared in
consultation with the BBC Continuing Education Advisory Council

Published by the British Broadcasting Corporation,
35 Marylebone High Street, London W1M 4AA
© Peter Russell 1979
First published 1979
ISBN 0 563 16360 7

Text set in 10/12pt VIP Sabon, printed and bound
in Great Britain at the Pitman Press, Bath

meditation
paths to tranquillity

by Peter Russell

Edited by Susan Paton

BRITISH BROADCASTING CORPORATION

Contents

1

The need for meditation

There is an old Buddhist saying that when the iron bird flies in the sky then the teaching of meditation will go to the West. Meditation has, of course, been taught in the West for many years as part of the Christian tradition, but it is only now, in an age when iron birds fly regularly through our skies, that many non-religious people are beginning to take meditation seriously. And many of the techniques of meditation that are attracting attention have indeed come from the East.

The word 'meditation' is used in a variety of different ways and has many different associations. For some, the word may imply concentrating the mind on some mental image, or possibly on the idea of nothing; for others, it may mean thinking about an idea, as when we meditate on the state of the economy. Meditation may be a form of devotion or prayer; it may mean an examination of one's internal thought processes, or simply a settling down of the mind into quietness. For some it could be sitting in a meadow on a summer afternoon letting the sun and birdsong carry you away; or it may mean a guided meditation in which a therapist asks a patient to imagine certain things happening to him. All these meanings and more have passed under the umbrella of 'meditation'. In this book we will look at meditation mainly as a technique for bringing the mind to a state of peace and quiet, and at some of the various ways in which this can be done.

The techniques discussed represent the different approaches to meditation which can be found in Britain today, and the specific techniques chosen are generally the most popular form of each type of meditation. We shall look at Transcendental Meditation as an example of a simple technique for bringing the mind to a state of complete quiet; at some of the main forms of Buddhist meditation; at the Dynamic Meditation of Bhagwan Shree Rajneesh; at more devotional practices, such as Baba Muktananda's Siddha Yoga; and at some of the meditations practised within the Christian Church.

Most people probably associate meditation with religion, and it is certainly true that most religious practices include meditation as an essential part of their teaching. We shall see, however, that it is not necessary to be religiously minded to meditate, nor to give up worldly things, as is often supposed. Today, meditation is being found valuable by ordinary, everyday people, many of whom may not be particularly religious, and may seem to be far more concerned with leading full and active lives, rather than retiring into a monastery. Meditation is now being practised as much by doctors, farmers, business executives, policemen, students, artists, university professors and secretaries as it is by the professionally religious. Just walking down a busy shopping street you will probably pass several people who regularly practise some technique of meditation.

Although meditation is gaining increased acceptance, it is still regarded as something slightly strange. Yoga was in the same situation ten years ago; many people recognized its value, but it was still thought to be a little cranky. Today very few people raise an eyebrow at the mention of yoga, it is almost part of the establishment; maybe in ten years' time, or even less, the same will be true of meditation.

The increased acceptance has come partly from the now considerable scientific research into meditation, and partly from the growing awareness that, as the pace of life increases, the ability to sit still now and again and be at peace and at one with the world becomes more and more urgent.

Bringing the mind to a state of peace and quiet is not always as easy as it sounds. Most people, if they were to sit down quietly and close their eyes would soon find that they had endless thoughts going round and round in their heads. The problem is, how do you persuade these continual 'butterfly' thoughts to stop coming? How do you come to that state of peace? As many people have found to their disappointment, merely trying to stop thoughts is not very helpful; you may well end up with the thought of how you wish you could stop thoughts, and so become even more frustrated.

This is where techniques of meditation are so valuable. They provide specific practices which help the mind to settle down and, ultimately, to arrive at a state of complete inner silence.

The actual techniques for doing this vary a lot. Some use special sounds called 'mantras', which, in techniques such as Transcendental Meditation, you may think quietly to yourself, and in other techniques you may chant or sing aloud. Some Buddhist meditations replace the mantra with an awareness of the breathing, just watching its steady rise and fall. Some meditations use visual images, such as the image of a vase or a candle flame. And in the more religious practices one may use the idea of God as a focus of meditation. Other methods are much more active and use the body as a means of meditation, as in the Dynamic Meditation of Bhagwan Shree Rajneesh, where people are deliberately energetic for a while in order to free themselves of some of the physical tensions they may have been carrying around. Yoga is another example of a physical practice which can become meditation. And so are the whirling dervishes of the Middle East who reach a silent meditative state of mind by pirouetting rapidly, often for hours at a time. Underlying all these approaches, however, is a common aim – to help the mind settle down and become still.

Since the workings of the mind and body are intimately connected, the quiet, relaxed mental state reached during meditation has corresponding effects on the body. The quieter the mind becomes, the more still and rested the body grows. This is borne out by the common experience that the quiet state of mind reached during meditation leaves a feeling of relaxation and refreshment. People generally find themselves coming back to activity with renewed energy and a zest for life.

Thus meditation has been found to be a very effective way of helping people to relax physically, and as such is being found valuable in enabling them to cope with the pressures and stresses of modern life.

The world of business is one area where one might not expect to find meditation, yet more and more companies are beginning to take a serious look at it. Although they do not always want to talk about it – presumably because they are wary of being associated with strange religious groups – many people in business are starting to meditate, and some companies are even offering to pay for employees to learn. Transcendental Meditation seems to be the principal technique being used, presumably because it is the least religious and the most adaptable to being taught in a business environment.

This interest on the part of the business world stems from its increasing concern with the effects of stress, particularly on health. In addition, there is also a growing anxiety about the ways in which stress can lead to abrasive personal relationships, dull the mind and contribute to misunderstandings between different sectors of industry.

Most techniques of meditation seem to be able to produce the exact opposite to the stress reaction. Whenever the body is faced with some emergency, is threatened, alarmed or put under pressure, it goes into a standard stress reaction, commonly known as the 'flight-or-fight response'. This reaction is so called because the body is being prepared for instant action – either to run for its life or to fight to the death. The heart rate immediately speeds up, the blood pressure increases, the breathing quickens, the muscles begin to tense and the skin starts to perspire. At the same time, sugar and other substances are released into the blood to provide the body with extra energy. Now, although this may be very useful in cases where there is a real physical emergency – if, for example, you were suddenly faced by a bull in a field, which looked as if it were about to charge, and you really needed every ounce of energy you could muster – the response has outlived much of its usefulness.

In daily life you are seldom in such extreme physical danger, yet you may still have the same reaction many times a day. Driving in city traffic produces the effect continuously. On the open road your heart rate may temporarily double every time you go to overtake another vehicle, yet the only physical actions you make are slight movements of the wrists and ankle. Dealing with a difficult customer on the phone, facing an irate boss, being criticized at home, all these and many other situations can result in the body reacting with the standard flight-or-fight response.

Because you may not actually run for your life or fight to the death in these situations, the body never works out the reaction naturally. Instead it stays wound up, only slowly returning to normal, and often taking an hour or more to do so. During this time you may well meet some other threat or pressure and get wound up again. The net effect of this continual over-arousal is that at the end of the day many people are in a permanent state of emergency, whether or not there is actually an emergency at hand. This is a condition that doctors call 'hypertension'.

When a person is in a state of permanent high arousal, the blood pressure remains high, the heart rate is higher than it should be and this in turn leads to many problems in the heart and circulation. Indeed, some cardiologists now believe that as much as ninety or ninety-five per cent of heart complaints are self-induced by the person who just goes on and on, keeping himself under continual pressure and ending up in a state of permanent over-arousal.

It is not only the heart which is affected by tension. Muscles which are continually tense may begin to ache, or develop symptoms such as fibrositis, and may also start contributing to bad body posture. The acidity of the stomach is upset, so that the stomach actually starts to digest itself, resulting eventually in stomach ulcers and other digestive complaints. The whole body generally becomes fatigued and feeble, and less able to cope with a bacterial infection or some other genuine emergency. The effects of stress and over-arousal are so widespread that they are thought to be a major factor in three-quarters of the cases faced by doctors in their surgeries.

What we need more than anything today is the ability to unwind. One of the standard ways of achieving this has been through the use of tranquillizers. However, giving drugs to reduce stress has two disadvantages. Firstly, there are always undesirable side effects. The chemicals concerned, in flowing through the blood stream, will affect all parts of the body, some of which may not need any treatment. From this mistreatment more problems may arise. Secondly, tranquillizers do not get to the root of the problem. They do not usually help the person who takes them to remain unflustered when under pressure; they merely treat the symptoms which occur when the person is too wound up.

The natural way for the body to deal with stress is to take rest. This is why we may feel more fatigued when we are too wound up; the body is saying 'I want some more rest'. If we ignore the symptoms and keep on going, the body may try to force its needs upon us, usually by collapsing. If we persist in ignoring the call, we may find ourselves heading for a more permanent form of rest. Some companies today have brought in a special type of leave called 'stress leave', in which the highly wound-up executive is sent off to somewhere like the Bahamas for a month or two to unwind. The trouble with this approach is that the company is losing a valuable person for a long period of time. In America today the problem has become so acute that in some areas they train two or three people to do the same job, working out that at any given time one of them should be well enough to do the job.

What people often need today is not more tranquillizers or long periods of leave, but methods of relaxing which can be incorporated into an active life. How many times have doctors said, 'I can give you a prescription for some drug or other, but I know and you know that what you really need is to relax'? This is why some doctors are now quietly suggesting to some patients that they take a more serious look at the techniques of meditation which are available. This does not mean to say that in many cases some form of physical treatment may not be necessary as well, but, if the treatment is combined with deep rest and relaxation, it would tend to be more effective and faster.

Since the 1970s there has been a rapidly growing interest in meditation from a scientific point of view, and by 1979 over four hundred scientific papers had been published on the various effects of the different systems of meditation. The technique that has been most thoroughly researched is Transcendental Meditation, which we shall be looking at more deeply in the next chapter. The general conclusion is that, within five minutes or so, meditation can produce a state of rest and relaxation considerably deeper than that of normal sleep.

In some respects meditation might be likened to sleep; the more wound up we are, the more tired we get and the more we need sleep. The better the sleep, the better we feel the next day, and the more effectively we are able to continue to act. Today's pressures often demand something in addition to normal sleep, and the extra-deep rest of meditation can have beneficial results for the body. The principle underlying this is the basic natural cycle of rest and activity; the more active we are, the deeper the state of rest we need to balance it.

In other respects, however, meditation is not like sleep, and it is not the same as having a quick nap. It is true that a quick nap in the middle of the afternoon can be very refreshing, but it generally does not have the same physiological and mental effects as a short period of meditation. The principal difference between meditation and sleep is that during meditation the mind is fully conscious – in some respects it is more conscious than in the normal waking state. The combination of being in a very deep state of physical and mental rest and, at the same time, being wide awake and conscious means that on coming out of meditation a person usually feels alert rather than sleepy or dozy, and ready to resume activity with renewed energy.

One of the most interesting areas of research has been into the brain activity of individuals who are meditating. Psychologists have discovered that the human brain shows patterns of activity that differ according to its state of consciousness. The brain of someone who is wide awake and mentally active shows a different pattern from that when it is at rest, and different patterns again occur during both sleep and dreams. A common finding with nearly all techniques of meditation is that, during the meditative state, the brain is in a very relaxed state, and the activity it produces is often similar to that of the borderline state between waking and sleeping. This is the state which we may often experience last thing at night and first thing in the morning, in which strange fleeting images pass before the mind's eye, and in which we sometimes lose contact with everyday reality. Ordinarily we pass through this state very quickly, often glimpsing it for only a few seconds, or half a minute. Meditation seems to produce the ability to linger in a similar state for ten or fifteen minutes at a time.

This borderline state of consciousness has always fascinated man. Many artists find that their inspiration comes from this relaxed but dreamy state; ninety per cent of all scientific breakthroughs have come during this state, and many other people have found that a solution to a pressing problem often flashes up just before going to sleep, or just after waking in the morning. We might, therefore, expect people who are meditating to experience some increase in creativity, and many have reported that they have found this is the case.

This does not necessarily imply that meditation is exactly the same as this transition period between wakefulness and sleep. The brain's activity may be similar, but there may also be subtle differences. In the personal experience of many meditators – and in the final analysis this is the real test – the mind is usually very much more alert and clear during meditation and, unless the person is particularly over-tired, does not have that hazy, dreamy quality found on the borderline of sleep.

When people are very tired, or have accumulated a 'sleep debt', they may well find themselves falling asleep in meditation – as they might while reading a book or watching television. This is a natural catching up on the part of the body, and afterwards meditation is usually much clearer. It may even sometimes be necessary to prescribe sleep for eighteen or twenty hours a day for perhaps a week to someone who is extremely over-wrought before attempting to teach meditation. Only after they have begun to unwind will it be possible to begin teaching them meditation or some other technique of relaxation.

I do not wish to imply that the only people who take up meditation are those who are chronically ill or exhausted. Most of those who start are ordinary, reasonably healthy, sane, fairly integrated individuals who simply want to get more out of life, feel a little more rested, clearer in their minds, be more open to other people, enjoy life more, know themselves a little better, have a deeper understanding of life and perhaps come closer to the divine. It is significant that about eighty per cent of those who start meditation come through the recommendation of friends.

Concern is often expressed that meditation, by relieving the effects of stress, might remove drive. This concern probably comes from a confusion between physiological stress in the sense of over-arousal, and stress in the sense of external pressure applied by the environment and by other people. It is certainly true that most of us need external pressure in one form or another to drive us on. It may be the demands of our job, of other people or of our superiors; the demands of time; social pressures; or simply the commitments we have set ourselves. The trouble is that these various external pressures may so tax the body that it becomes physiologically stressed – the blood pressure remains high, the muscles tense and so on. This aspect of stress is certainly not necessary for drive, and in many cases hinders effective performance. What we really need is the ability to live in a world which is full of pressures, and to be able to cope with these pressures adequately without driving the body into permanent states of over-arousal, with all the tragic consequences which can follow. In this respect, meditation, by bringing the body back into balance, is helping it to cope more effectively with the day-to-day pressures of a busy life.

Some people might suspect that they get as much from having a couple of stiff whiskies as they would from meditation. Certainly alcohol can help you relax, and it can often stop a lot of those worrying thoughts which go round and round in your head, but it does not seem to have the same effect as meditation on the physiology or on the consciousness. One of the basic characteristics of alcohol is that it depresses mental functioning. It is common to think of alcohol as something that stimulates us and gets us going, but from the neurological point of view it really does the opposite. What happens is that it depresses the functioning of the brain and, in doing so, slightly reduces control. We become less inhibited, feel more free and easy and can get up and go. This is, in fact, quite different from meditation, during which the brain and mind are becoming more rested, and the meditator does not want to be moving about the whole time but to be sitting still with a relatively quiet mind. That the two have opposite effects is borne out by the fact that those who practise meditation generally agree that it is more difficult to do after a couple of stiff whiskies.

Another common query is about exercise. Cannot jogging or a game of squash be just as relaxing? Physical exercise is certainly valuable, particularly for those who spend much of the day sitting or standing in one position. For those whose work does not enable them to move around, some of the muscles stay permanently contracted. Exercise performs the useful function of alternately expanding and contracting many of the muscles. Exercise also gives the blood a chance to carry away waste products and to replenish the oxygen supply, and, if the exercise is intense, it can be very valuable for the heart and lungs. This is why physical exercise is so refreshing. But we do also need periods of complete inactivity when both body and mind are given total rest. Thus exercise does not replace the deep rest of meditation – nor does meditation replace exercise.

In addition to its many physiological effects, meditation also has many effects on the mind. Indeed, in the past it was practised largely for its mental and spiritual values. From a psychological point of view, the basis of all meditation techniques may be thought of as a modification of the process of attention.

There is an old Zen Buddhist story of a man who approached a master and asked for the highest wisdom.

'Attention,' the master replied.

'Is that all?' asked the man. 'Is there nothing more?'

'Attention. Attention,' replied the master.

'Well,' remarked the man, 'I don't see much depth in that.'

'Attention. Attention. Attention,' the master replied.

Half-angered, the man demanded, 'What is attention, anyway?'

'Attention means attention,' answered the master gently.

All techniques of meditation involve a shift of attention, and generally lead to an awareness of aspects of mental processes of which the meditator was previously unaware or only dimly aware. In Transcendental Meditation, for example, you sit down quietly and attend in a passive manner to a meaningless sound repeated silently within, turning the attention a hundred and eighty degrees away from the outside world of sensory experience on to the subtler, underlying levels of thinking. As with many meditation techniques, there is a shift from an active 'doing' mode of attention to a passive 'letting things be'. In other techniques you may deliberately hold the attention to a chosen mental image, eliminating or inhibiting distracting thoughts. Some techniques use the way of devotion, surrendering up all individual desires, and putting the attention on some higher goal. In other techniques you simply attend as fully as possible to whatever it is you are doing. However varied the techniques may seem, the key is attention.

The common goal of all these techniques is to arrive at a state of inner mental silence, a state in which experience, as we normally know it, ceases. This is why, when the state is first encountered, it often seems one of emptiness – hence the Buddhists sometimes call it the Void. Hindus call it *Samadhi*, meaning literally a 'still mind'. In Zen meditation it is called *Ming* (self-knowledge), and in the Taoist traditions of China it is sometimes called *Tso-Wang* (sitting with no thoughts). As well as being a state of mental silence it is also said to be a most fulfilling and enjoyable state.

It is said to be a state in which the true self is known. The thoughts, images and experience with which the mind normally identifies fade away, and the meditator ceases to think 'I am this' or 'I am that', but begins to feel that simply 'I am'. Eventually even this awareness of the self drops off, and the person is said to be in a state of pure being in which he or she feels united with the whole of humanity, all of life and even with the whole of creation.

How an individual interprets such an experience depends upon his cultural background and religious inclinations. A Christian might describe it as the experience of the Godhead, or perhaps as the essence of Christ; a Buddhist might talk of it as the Buddha nature; and a Hindu as Brahman. A person with no particular orientation, on the other hand, might describe it as a state of pure, unmanifest consciousness. The actual name or personal interpretation given to this state does not really matter so much as the influence this state has on the life of the individual who experiences it. Having experienced such a unity and possibly gained the realization that at the deepest level we are all 'one and the same', people have found themselves spontaneously becoming more loving and compassionate in their daily activity. And this, most teachers would agree, is the real value of meditation in the world today.

2

Transcendental Meditation

Transcendental Meditation (or TM, as it is usually abbreviated) is probably the most popular technique of meditation being taught in Britain today. TM has its origins in India, and claims that its history can be traced back several thousands of years, though just how old it is no-one really knows. We in the West first heard about it in the late fifties when the Maharishi (Maharishi Mahesh Yogi, to give him his full title) left India and started travelling around the world teaching the technique.

Maharishi himself had, for twelve years, been a close student of the renowned Indian teacher Brahmananda Saraswati, who occupied the position of Shankarcharya of North India – our nearest equivalent probably being the Archbishop of Canterbury. After his master's death, Maharishi decided that the technique of Transcendental Meditation should be practised not just by a few monks in Himalayan retreats, but by everyone. It was something that the whole world should benefit from, and consequently he set out to spread the technique as widely as possible.

It first really began to catch on in a big way after 1967 when the Beatles and various other public figures took up the technique and even went out to India themselves to study it further. They claimed that TM had turned them away from drugs and completely changed their lives – claims which the public press, with its characteristic gift for sensationalism, managed to make the most out of. Since then, TM has been growing steadily, and now, in 1979, claims to have taught over one and a half million people around the world – including about one hundred thousand in the United Kingdom.

As well as being the most popular technique it is probably also the simplest. One of the Maharishi's main achievements has been to strip away as much as possible of the religious trappings and dogma which so often surround meditation, and to bring out the essence of the practice. His prime aim is simply to teach people a technique of meditation. He does not ask them to adopt any particular spiritual beliefs, join any religion or accept any particular philosophies. Christians, Jews, Hindus and atheists alike can practise the technique. Nor does he ask people to change their life styles; one does not have to become a vegetarian or a particularly upright citizen to gain benefit from the technique.

At a first glance, one of the outstanding aspects of Maharishi's teaching is that he appears to have reversed many of the standard

opposite: Maharishi Mahesh Yogi

ideas about meditation. Most people believe that meditation is a very difficult process and requires intense concentration. Maharishi tries to show that with TM, at least, the opposite is true, and that the technique itself is remarkably simple, and does not require any great effort. Indeed, the very act of concentration tends to upset the process of meditation. With TM the less you *try* to meditate the more likely you are to succeed.

He also claims that anybody can meditate, whatever their life style, disposition or moral standards. In many other traditions it is felt that you should become a 'good' person first, and then, having purified your life, you would be ready to take up meditation. Maharishi claims that the opposite is the case with TM; one of the long-term effects of meditation is that you spontaneously become a better citizen: a good life follows as a result of meditation rather than as a prerequisite for it.

He also believes that the same basic technique can be taught to all types of people, whether they be artists, or scientists, male or female, old or young, clever or stupid, introvert or extrovert. Teachers of other types of meditation might not agree with this generalization of the technique, but it has certainly streamlined the teaching, and allowed the technique to be made much more widely available.

Nor does TM advocate any renunciation of wordly affairs. The actual practice of meditation does involve a temporary withdrawal from the world, but it is a withdrawal in order to return to activity much more effectively. It is seen as a recharging of mental and physical resources. Far from being a withdrawal from activity, the technique aims to enhance daily activity by balancing it with a corresponding degree of rest.

Those who take up TM do not meditate for the experience of meditation itself but for the effects that it has on their daily lives. The basic principle is that if the body is more rested and the mind calm and clear, then you will be able to act more effectively, get more done and enjoy life more. Many people also find that they become much less harassed by everyday events. A commonly quoted example is driving, where many people report that they can deal with traffic snarl-ups, or other drivers cutting in, without getting over-wrought and distressed. One lady I met reported how the Transport Manager of her company had found that her rate of petrol consumption had decreased after she learned TM – presumably because she was not revving up at the lights so much and was generally taking things more easily.

Most people who practise TM do so for about twenty minutes twice a day, usually first thing in the morning and again around the late afternoon or early evening, at the end of the normal working day.

The way in which the TM technique works is to allow the mind to settle down to quieter and quieter levels of thinking until it eventually becomes completely silent. It is not so much a controlling of the mind as a relaxing of it. To do this you do not need to sit cross-legged, or in any strange yoga position; you are merely asked to sit in a comfortable chair with your eyes closed. It is recommended that you do not lie down, but this is only so that you do not become drowsy. It is also recommended that you do not meditate after a large meal. The reason is not that it is dangerous to meditate after a meal, but simply that meditation tends to be dull and less effective when the stomach is busy digesting food.

To help the mind settle down to a quiet state, Transcendental Meditation makes use of what are called 'mantras'. These are words, or rather sounds, which have no particular meaning as far as the meditator is concerned (although most of them do have some meaning in Sanskrit, an ancient Indian language). In TM the meaninglessness of the mantra is very important. If you were to choose a meaningful sound such as the word 'telephone' you would soon be thinking of whom you had to call, who rang yesterday, whether a certain person was going to phone today, whether you had paid the bill, what about an extension and so on. With a meaningless sound this will not happen, and the mind can settle down much more easily.

Not any meaningless sound will do. It is obviously going to be more conducive to the mind to settle down to a calm, quiet state if the sound is soothing rather than jarring. The sound of finger-nails scraping down glass, for example, may not contain much meaning, but for most of us it does not have a very soothing quality, and would not be a very suitable sound for meditation. The sounds used in TM are ones which have been chosen for their soothing natures and generally do not contain harsh syllables or consonants.

Although considerable fuss is made of the mantra in TM, it is not the most important aspect of the practice. Far more crucial is the technique of using the mantra, and it is with this that the instruction is mainly concerned. The traditional Indian idea is that you should sit down and continuously repeat the mantra to yourself as some form of mental chant. This is not the case with TM. You are instructed to think the mantra in a completely effortless way, not trying to make a continual repetition, nor trying to focus the attention on the mantra. The correct attitude of mind in TM is very much one of just letting things flow: a passive awareness rather than any control or concentration.

Maharishi's revolutionary attitude towards concentration stems from his equally revolutionary explanation of how the mind works. Most people have noticed that their minds frequently wander from one thought to another, never being still on one idea, let alone completely silent; they present a continually changing panorama of thoughts and images. In the past it has been assumed that it must be the nature of the mind to wander, and that if the mind is to be brought to a state of calm it must be controlled. Indian writings have summed this up by likening the mind to a monkey in a tree continually jumping from branch to branch. Monkeys, it is said, are naturally mischievous creatures, and the only way you can keep one still is to tie it down. Similarly with the mind, it has to be 'tied down', and so a vast range of practices have developed with the intention of controlling the mind. Some of these aim at holding the attention to one thought, whereas others try to keep the mind empty of all thoughts. Whatever the technique, it is thought that effort and discipline are essential if any success is to be gained.

Maharishi takes a different view, and suggests that the mind is wandering not because it loves to wander but because it is looking for something, and that something is satisfaction. Just as a wise monkey-catcher realizes that the monkey is leaping around because it is looking for something – more bananas, perhaps – and quietly brings the monkey down, simply by placing a banana at the foot of the tree, so Maharishi believes that once the mind appreciates that there is an inner source of satisfaction, it will begin to settle down of its own accord without any effort or control. The quieter the mind becomes, the more satisfaction is found, and the less effort is needed to keep it still. Indeed, any effort generally makes the mind more active, and as far as TM is concerned, tends to bring the person out of the meditative state.

Of all meditation techniques, TM has undoubtedly been subjected to more scientific investigation than any other. To date, more than two hundred scientific papers have been written on various aspects of the technique and its effects. As far as the body is concerned, the general finding is that during TM it very rapidly sinks into a state of deep relaxation. The breathing slows down and softens, muscles relax, the heart rate decreases, and there is a decrease in blood pressure in those for whom it is already high. These changes, coupled with the finding that hormones and other chemicals in the blood associated with stress are decreasing, support the hypothesis that the technique is producing the exact opposite to the stress reaction. Studies suggest that the level of relaxation reached during TM is deeper than during normal sleep. Oxygen consumption during meditation may fall by fifteen to twenty per cent, and sometimes by as much as fifty per cent, whereas in sleep it generally falls only by about ten per cent.

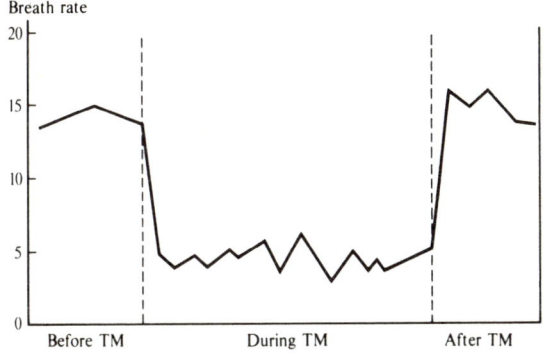

Decrease in breath rate during TM

There has also been considerable research into the activity of the brain during TM. One particularly interesting finding, which so far has been reported only in the course of practising the TM technique, though undoubtedly it occurs with other techniques of meditation, is a synchronization of the electrical activity in the left and right sides of the brain. It is generally thought that the left side of the brain is more concerned with verbal tasks such as reading, writing and speech, whereas the right is more concerned with visual and spatial functions. Most people tend to use the functions associated with the left side of the brain more than with those of the right. This may be partly a cultural effect, reflecting the past bias in education towards the three R's.

23

As a person goes deeper into meditation, the brain activity not only shows a very relaxed pattern, but also begins to show very similar waves coming from the left and right sides. The two sides of the brain would appear to be coming more into balance. This suggests there is a much greater flow of information through the millions of fibres which connect the two halves, and also that as a result of meditation, people might be able to use the right side of their brain more fully, and integrate this with the functioning of the left side.

Other scientists have been looking at the psychological effects of Transcendental Meditation, although these are often much harder to pin down. The general finding is that in the long term TM decreases anxiety, depression and neurosis, and leads to greater self-confidence and personal esteem. Other tests have suggested that the meditating person may be a more stable individual and better able to survive the ups and downs of the changing world. These sort of effects are, however, long-term, and you should not expect to notice them immediately (although a few people do). They are much more likely to become apparent six months or a year after learning the technique.

Because Maharishi has generally presented TM in a non-religious way, and also because it is a technique which people can practise on their own, Transcendental Meditation has found increasing acceptance in many diverse fields, from big business through to monasteries. One of its most interesting uses has been in prisons.

In the U.S.A., TM has been taught in about a dozen prisons, and the most dramatic results have been in Folsom Penitentiary in California. This is a maximum security prison for extreme offenders, mostly murderers. A few years ago, two hundred and fifty of the fifteen hundred inmates were taught Transcendental Meditation, with very marked, immediate results. The murder rate inside the prison dropped dramatically, from about ten per year down to about one per year. Of the men who had learnt TM, thirty were released one year later, and so far only one ended up coming back, and he only came back for not reporting as required to his probation officer; in the normal way eighty per cent of those released eventually end up inside again. As a result of this and other programmes, the TM technique is being increasingly considered as a way of rehabilitating prisoners. Judges have actually sentenced people to lesser terms on the condition that they practise TM.

Another interesting result found in Folsom Penitentiary is that the prisoners were beginning to become involved in academic activities, some of them taking degrees inside the prison. They were also getting much more involved in sports and creative activities. One prisoner reported that since he had been practising TM, he had 'never felt so free in my life, even though I'm behind fifteen-foot walls'.

At the other end of the social spectrum there are a growing number of monks, nuns and priests who have learnt Transcendental Meditation. Initially this might seem very surprising. Most orders of monks and nuns have their own techniques of meditation and would hardly be thought to need any new techniques, particularly something with Eastern connections. Most of the monks and nuns who have learnt TM have reported that the technique is basically very similar to the meditation beliefs buried deep within the Christian religion; techniques such as the Prayer of the Heart and the Prayer of Simplicity, which we shall look at a little more in the last chapter. They felt that anything that could possibly supplement their own techniques and experience of meditation was worth investigating. In many cases they were also interested in gaining a greater understanding of other traditions and uncovering the common truths which underlie all forms of meditation and spiritual practice.

As with other techniques of meditation, TM can be seen as a means of spiritual development as well as a system of relaxation. This aspect is normally underplayed by teachers of the technique, who feel that people may misunderstand the idea of spiritual development and so be put off starting. However, the states of consciousness which are claimed to develop as a result of TM bear close similarities to the states of consciousness reached by other techniques, and to those states described by mystical and spiritual writings the world over.

The deepest state reached by means of the TM technique is known as transcendental consciousness. This corresponds to the state in which normal mental activity has died away and the mind is left completely still. Paradoxical as it might seem, the meditator is still fully awake in this state: he is conscious, though there is nothing to be conscious of. One is said to have transcended (that is, gone beyond) the normal active levels of the mind. This is also why the technique itself is called Transcendental Meditation.

In addition to being a very restful and peaceful state, transcendental consciousness is also valuable in that it puts a person in contact with the true self, free from the boundaries of the ego, and gives a sense of unity with the rest of creation. A long-term aim of TM is to live this state of inner unity throughout one's daily life. This is what Maharishi refers to as 'Cosmic Consciousness'. It may be defined as maintaining an awareness of the experience of unity found deep in meditation, no matter what activity one is engaged in, whether it be eating, talking, driving a car, working on a problem, or even dreaming or fast asleep. This state is also commonly referred to as 'enlightenment', and although the precise descriptions may vary a little, it is the common goal of all meditation techniques.

The basic instruction in TM is fairly straightforward. It is usually done in four lessons, spread over four consecutive days, each lesson lasting between one and one and a half hours. The instruction is always carried out by qualified teachers of TM, of whom there are now nearly a thousand around Britain.

Introductory talks giving people some insight into the possible benefits of TM are now given in most major towns. This is followed a few days later by a preparatory talk, going more into the theory of meditation and the practical details of instruction. After this there is a short private interview between teacher and student.

The first session of instruction is always conducted personally on a one-to-one basis. It is preceded by a short ceremony in Sanskrit lasting about five minutes. This ceremony is part of the Indian tradition of teaching, and is said to recall the lineage of teachers who, over the centuries, have handed down the technique from one to another. Naturally, people are sometimes concerned that they are being asked to participate in a ceremony with Indian origins. It is not, however, something the student is closely involved in. Its purpose is to remind the teacher of his relationship to the tradition as a whole. This tends to reduce any ego involvement on the part of the teacher and makes him or her more neutral.

After the first instruction you meditate at home twice a day, and over the next three days receive further instruction and explanation of the practice, and, perhaps, personal guidance on any queries or difficulties.

Because it is very easy for the new meditator to introduce some slight distortion or effort into the practice without realizing it, he or she is normally requested to return to see the teacher periodically for what is called 'checking'. In the beginning, this may mean meeting with the teacher once every three or four weeks. Later it will probably be once every few months. As well as keeping the technique of meditation in trim and ensuring that the meditator gets the maximum from the practice, these meetings also give the new meditator a chance to understand more about his experiences.

In Britain, Transcendental Meditation is taught under the auspices of the Maharishi International College, an educational charity. Like most other meditation organizations, they make a charge for teaching meditation, and this money is used mostly in setting off administrative costs, the upkeep of teaching premises and the promotion of the technique.

Charging for meditation is sometimes criticized on the grounds that spiritual practices have traditionally been given out free. This may have been true in the Church, but, in Britain, the Church is one of the largest landlords, and as a result of its considerable income can afford to give such services more freely. Apart from the Christian Church, nearly all organizations teaching meditation make some charge or ask for contributions in one form or another.

Instead of charging people by the session, the TM organization asks for a single contribution at the start of instruction. This covers all the initial teaching sessions, and regular follow-up sessions as long as a person needs them (probably two or three years). Making an initial charge like this is often a burden on some people, particularly those in lower income groups, although it does mean that people are more likely to come back for the 'free' follow-up sessions. In an attempt to make this as equitable as possible, the suggested contribution is varied according to individual means.

Does this mean, as the press would have us believe, that Maharishi himself is earning a large fortune from the movement? The answer from anyone who has known Maharishi is emphatically 'No'. Maharishi still sees himself as a monk and refuses to have any personal possessions, apart from the sandals on his feet and the white dhoti which he wears around him. The contributions are all used in one way or another in the furtherance of the TM movement – though it might be objected that the money is not always spent as wisely as it could be. No individual, however, is making a fortune out of the movement, and in most cases teachers manage to live on a bare subsistence income.

Because Maharishi's aim is to make meditation as widely available as possible, a large organization has inevitably sprung up to oversee and co-ordinate the teaching around the world. As with all large organizations, this has involved the growth of bureaucracy and hierarchical structures of responsibility which many people find off-putting.

Some people also feel that the organization has lost touch with the 'grass-roots' meditator, particularly in the lavishly printed hand-outs and excessively optimistic claims about some of the effects of the technique. At the root of Maharishi's thinking is the idea that if more people were to practise meditation the world would become a more peaceful one. One of his important contributions has been to suggest that each individual can himself do something about the furtherance of world peace, and he is thus encouraging people to think more about their own role in the world. From this have grown various claims of the dawning of an age of enlightment, the establishment of an ideal society and even the establishment of a world government. The idea of this world government is not to take over from ordinary governments, but, by raising people's consciousness, to improve the quality of life generally – a government through consciousness rather than economics or politics. Some people find these ideas bear little connection with their own view of reality, and those who start TM usually do so without understanding or being particularly concerned about this side of the movement. It is usually something that they come to understand later once they have become more familiar with Maharishi's thinking.

To find out details of the various classes which are held throughout Britain and addresses of local centres, contact:

Maharishi International College, Roydon Hall,
Seven Mile Lane, East Peckham,
Nr Tonbridge, Kent
Telephone: Maidstone 812121.

Further reading

CAMPBELL, Anthony *Seven states of consciousness* Gollancz, 1973.
RUSSELL, Peter *The TM technique: an introduction to Transcendental Meditation and the teachings of Maharishi Mahesh Yogi* Routledge and Kegan Paul, n.e. 1978.

Dynamic Meditation

Dynamic Meditation is the name usually given to a specific set of meditation techniques taught by the Indian teacher Bhagwan Shree Rajneesh. Like Maharishi, Rajneesh has attempted to secularize meditation so that anyone can take it up, whatever their religion or cultural background.

Rajneesh himself belongs to no particular religious tradition and had no guru or spiritual master of his own. For nine years he was professor of philosophy at two Indian colleges, later resigning in order to devote his life to the inner development of others. He began integrating academic philosophy with his own inner experiences of meditation, and as he travelled around India talking on the subject, soon began to gather a large number of students. Although Rajneesh has never been outside India, thousands of Westerners have been attracted to his techniques. As a result, numerous Rajneesh Meditation Centres have opened up in many parts of the world.

Unlike Maharishi, Rajneesh does not advocate the same techniques for everyone. Most people usually start with Dynamic Meditation, but then might move on to any one of a vast spectrum of techniques, ranging from yoga and Buddhist meditations to movement, dance and even to Western techniques of Gestalt therapy. He believes that different people have different inner needs at different times, and that these needs must all be attended to before meditation can be complete. Coming from no particular tradition, he attempts to incorporate in his teachings what he sees as the most valid aspects of all traditions, and happily integrates Yoga, Christianity, Zen Buddhism, Sufism, Taoism, Hinduism and Tantra with Einstein, Wittengstein, Russell, Hegel and Marx.

The ultimate aim of his meditations is the same as TM, and all other forms of meditation – that is, to discover that state of consciousness we call enlightenment. He agrees that as part of this process the mind must be allowed to settle down to a state of quiet, but feels that most people, being wrapped up in the activities and tensions of the world, cannot simply sit down and relax.

Meditation, he points out, is a 'non-doing'. Because we are so used to 'doing' throughout our lives, any attempt to *practise* meditation becomes another form of doing. If people are told 'just relax', they do not know what 'to do', and a conflict often arises as how to relax. In TM this difficulty is overcome by a technique which takes the mind off the whole subject of relaxation, and yet in

opposite: Bhagwan Shree Rajneesh

itself has a relaxing effect. Rajneesh, on the other hand, deals with the problem by first deliberately making people very active, and then, once the tension has been brought to a peak, relaxation is allowed to come by simply 'letting go'. The various exercises used to make the meditator more active are what Rajneesh calls Dynamic Meditation. Strictly speaking, it is not meditation in the sense of inner silence: it is, rather, a springboard from which to experience true meditation.

Dynamic Meditation usually consists of five stages: chaotic breathing, catharsis, 'hoo', stopping dead and dance.

Chaotic breathing

Dynamic Meditation starts off with ten minutes of very fast breathing through the nose – as deep and as fast as possible. This uses the whole body to force the air in and out. You are instructed to throw yourself into it as completely as possible, just taking the breath in and throwing it out, as vigorously, as deeply and as intensely as possible.

The thinking behind this is that breathing is intimately connected with our states of mind and everything we do. When we are angry we have a particular rhythm of breathing; when we are in love a totally different rhythm comes to us. A child breathes in a certain way, and a fearful person in a different way. The aim of chaotic breathing is to destroy past patterns of tension in the breath and to release repressed emotions. On a physiological level fast, deep breathing puts more oxygen into the blood, and this can make you feel much more alive and vital – although if overdone, it can make you feel dizzy as well, but perhaps this is all part of the chaos. This meditation is done to music, and after ten minutes the mood of the music changes and people move into the second stage.

Catharsis

You now do whatever comes into your mind. You simply allow the body and lungs to express any emotions which may have bubbled up to the surface during the chaotic breathing. Some people may feel frustrated, others exhausted, yet others perhaps full of energy. People may want to weep and cry; some to dance around, leap about or just be 'crazy'. Others may want to be like babies, and just crawl around the floor; some to shout and be angry with a friend or loved one. Some may simply want to scream. To an outsider, this can appear to be a very frightening phase of the meditation, but those who are taking part seem to experience it as a welcome release from their tensions.

Many of us have become so restrained in our emotions that we do not normally let them fly so readily. We have been taught to laugh only when appropriate, to scream only in private (if at all), not to dance or leap about in public and to hold back our tears. Anyone who does not conform in this way we tend to regard as a bit 'crazy'. Yet most of us probably could do with a little more 'craziness' in our lives, and these ten minutes of catharsis can be valuable in helping to express, in a harmless way, some of the emotions locked up inside.

'Hoo'

The third stage of Dynamic Meditation is based upon an old Sufi meditation. You chant the word 'hoo' fast and loudly for ten minutes. Your arms are raised above the head, and you jump up and down, landing hard on the soles of your feet with the intention of 'beating the sound down into the pelvic area'.

The idea here is that the whole of the pelvic area has become a common area of physiological block and tension, mainly because of its association with sex. Although we have moved into a much more permissive society, sex is still a somewhat taboo subject, and this is reflected in people's attitude to the pelvic area of their bodies. This 'hoo' exercise is intended to free some of those blocks.

Stopping dead

After the 'hoo' section the music suddenly stops, and so do you. No matter what position you are in you must stop completely and hold that position for ten minutes. This part of the meditation is derived from a technique used earlier by a Western teacher, Gurdjieff, and its aim is to allow you simply to be yourself, and to be aware of any feelings of change within. You should not *do* anything: no movement, no desiring, just remaining in the here and now, witnessing whatever is happening.

It may sound easy, but this is probably the most difficult part of all. Indeed, many people would argue that it is impossible to carry out such an exercise properly if you are not already enlightened. Rajneesh, however, seems to believe that it is possible, and that the preceding stages of the meditation make it that much easier. It is at this stage that the mind may settle down into a silent meditation.

Dance

The last stage is dance. For ten minutes you dance gently around the room, expressing any feelings which have come through the meditation. The aim is to synthesize and integrate the previous stages, not just mentally but with the body and emotions.

All of the above stages are done blindfolded. This is partly so that you are not put off by all the strange things that other people might be doing around you; its value is also that, because everyone else is blindfolded and cannot see you either, you will probably feel less inhibited and will allow your expressions and feelings to flow out all the more freely.

Some people might be concerned that this deliberate release of inhibitions and suppressed energy might lead them into situations which they could not manage. One might, for example, uncover a repressed feeling of sadness, and not having fully released it during the session, go back into the world feeling emotionally disturbed. Some teachers of Dynamic Meditation admitted that in *exceptional* circumstances this could happen, although they thought it was extremely rare. Most of them are themselves people who are trained in group work and therapeutic techniques, and are used to coping with people who have emotional difficulties. They felt that on the rare occasions when somebody did feel uncomfortable after a session they could spot it immediately, and help the person through it before they left. A reliable guide is, as with all meditations, very valuable, and you should therefore go along to a recognised centre rather than trying it on your own. And if it does not feel right for you, you do not have to do it.

Dynamic Meditation is only the beginning for Rajneesh's students; there are many other techniques that he teaches. The *Nataraj*, for example, consists of forty minutes' dancing. The meditator allows the unconscious to take over completely, dancing without any plan or control, just a total involvement in the music. This is followed by twenty minutes of lying down, completely still, allowing the vibrations of the dancing to continue flowing inside.

There is a whirling meditation derived from the dervish dance of the Sufis. The meditators whirl around on the spot, eyes open, body loose, arms extended and the mind out of focus. They start slowly, building up speed as they go, spinning faster and faster. This may be done for about half an hour, although true dervishes can keep it up for seven or eight hours at a time.

In another meditation known as *Nada Brahma*, derived from an old Tibetan technique, the meditator hums quietly, sitting in a relaxed position with the eyes closed for about thirty minutes. The idea is that after about half an hour a point will come where he is just a listener. The humming will be happening by itself.

Other meditations involve the visualization of lights; abandoned laughter (it is recommended that you try five minutes' laughter every morning upon wakening – it may change your whole approach to life); and speaking in total gibberish, with the intention of breaking up the pattern of continual verbalization.

In addition to these general meditations, Rajneesh is constantly devising new techniques, and incorporating other practices into his teaching. He usually selects specific practices for different students according to what he feels is right for them at the time. He may tell one person to suck a piece of linen for ten hours a day, another to look at himself in the mirror, another to start hitting a pillow, another to laugh continuously, another to cry continuously, another to undergo some form of psychotherapy and another to take up Transcendental Meditation.

Many of the people who get deeply involved with Rajneesh's meditations feel, at some time or another, that they need to go out to India and spend some time with Rajneesh himself. At his centre in Poona, near Bombay, followers can listen to him lecturing, and also get personal guidance from him about specific techniques of meditation. Many of the people who go there are themselves Indians and Rajneesh has established the custom of lecturing for one month in English, and then lecturing for the next month in the local language (so anyone thinking of visiting should first check that it is an 'English' month).

Those who make the trip to India often come back wearing orange, with a new name and a small photograph of Rajneesh hung around their necks. These changes are what Rejneesh calls the taking of *Sannyas*. In most Indian traditions this is seen as a form of social renunciation. The *Sannyasin* is one who has given up all wordly affairs. Rajneesh views it slightly differently, seeing it as giving up attachment to the world, but not renouncing worldly activity itself.

The first thing he does is to give the student a new name, usually in the ancient Indian language of Sanskrit. A name is chosen with an appropriate meaning to the person concerned. Thus someone may be given a name meaning 'joyful love', if Rajneesh feels that it is appropriate. In this respect the changing of names is somewhat similar to the original Christian practice of baptism, new names being given on initiation into the Christian Church, the name chosen reflecting an aspect of the individual – 'Peter', for example, being given to signify the strength of a rock. The intention behind Rajneesh's giving of a new name is that it should help a student forget his or her connections with the past, and identify less strongly with the superficial levels of ego. Some of Rajneesh's followers also feel it is important to have a name with a meaningful connection, rather than just a name chosen because it sounds nice.

The second requirement in taking *Sannyas* is to wear only orange – or, more specifically, to wear the colours of the rising sun, which effectively means anything from yellow to a rust or wine colour. The rising sun is said to symbolize warmth, healing and the dawn of a new life, and these colours have always been traditionally worn by Indian monks.

The aim here again is to help break identification with the past. Most people draw a strong sense of their personality from the clothes they wear, whether it be blue jeans, bowler hat and pinstripes, leather jacket and studs, mink coats or some official uniform. With many people the identification is so strong that if they were asked to wear something completely different they would resist the change very strongly. Rajneesh's idea is that by changing clothes and wearing only one colour, you change your attitude towards yourself. It is hoped that you will begin to give up some of your earlier conditioning as to the sort of person you feel yourself to be. Also, by limiting dress to one colour only, it is intended that you become less aware of clothing, and begin to respond more openly and with an inner sense of who you really are.

Some Rajneesh followers stand out a mile in their orange clothes. Dressed in Indian smocks and cotton trousers, they are reminiscent of the hippies of the sixties. Others, however, manage to dress so carefully and tastefully that you would not notice they are only wearing orange. Obviously it is much easier for women to get away with this, but I have also met several people in the business world who, through a careful choice of shades, have managed to satisfy

Rajneesh's requirements and yet still be dressed smartly enough to mingle unobtrusively with their fellow executives.

Whether or not the taking of a new name and the wearing of orange do indeed release one from an identification with the past is an open question. Some would argue that it is merely a superficial symbol of giving up one's conditioning, and that the real change can come only through the inner shift of consciousness which comes with prolonged practice of meditation. There is also the danger that one might give up one form of social identity only to take on another – that of being a Rajneesh follower – in which case the ego has shifted but it has not been freed.

The third requirement in taking *Sannyas* is to wear a *Mala*. The *Mala* consists of a necklace of 108 small beads, and from it is hung a small picture of Rajneesh. To many this might suggest an idolization of the teacher – although this is something in which Rajneesh himself claims not to be interested. Some of his followers say that it reminds them of him as a teacher; others regard it merely as a symbol of their connection to his teaching, much as Christians may wear a crucifix around their necks.

Ultimately, the three requirements must also be transcended. If a person is to receive a true enlightenment, there must come a time when he can throw away his orange clothes and *Mala*, and feel unattached to any particular name. Rajneesh himself very much agrees with this, saying that he is only there to help, and not to act as a source of dependence, otherwise the student is going to miss the goal, which is one of total liberation. He uses the old Zen Buddhist analogy of pointing to the moon. If your goal is to go to the moon, then don't hold on to the finger which is doing the pointing, or you will lose the goal. In the same way the various *Sannyas* point in the direction of a decreased bondage to the ego, but if that goal is really to be achieved, they must not themselves be clung to.

There are several centres in England which hold regular Dynamic Meditation sessions – usually every day, sometimes twice a day. The organization also runs special beginner sessions on some evenings when the basic stages of Dynamic Meditation are taught.

For more details of Rajneesh centres in England and of the courses available, contact:

Kalptaru, 10a Belmont Street, London NW1.
Telephone: 01–485 3216/4206

Further reading

Nearly every talk which Rajneesh gives is recorded, transcribed and edited into books. As a result, the Rajneesh organization has probably published more books than any other meditation group. To date there are about sixty books published, all of them of Rajneesh's teachings, and they vary from discourses on Jesus to Sufism, Zen Buddhism and Tantric Yoga. A full list of publications can be obtained from the above address. The best introductory book is:

RAJNEESH, Bhagwan S. *Meditation: the art of ecstasy* Harper and Row, paperback 1976. Available from Kalptaru above.

4

Buddhist Meditation

Buddhism was founded by a man called Gotama Siddhartha, the son of a noble family living in Northern India around 500 B.C. In his youth he became aware of the futility of a superficial social life and of excessive philosophical debates, and realized that the most important thing was 'right living'. Eventually he abandoned his home and family, and went in search of spiritual teachers who could give him instruction in yoga, meditation and right living. Tradition has it that after trying many different paths he finally achieved enlightenment (*bodhi*) while sitting under a tree, and thus became a *buddha* ('an enlightenened one'). The question then arose as to whether he should keep to himself the truths he had discovered or teach them to others. Eventually he decided to go out and teach, and spent the rest of this life trying to help others reach a state of enlightenment.

Nothing of what he taught was written down until about four hundred years later in a Ceylonese text known as the Pali Canon; before that time Buddhist teachings were handed down by word of mouth. As a result, no-one really knows for sure what the Buddha himself taught, and during the four hundred years which elapsed many different branches and sects developed. Buddhism is not, however, a dogmatic religion, and most sects are open to the teachings of other sects – and also to the teaching of the other major world religions. The basic aim throughout Buddhism is the development of the individual – to help a person gain liberation from the physical world (the world of suffering) by freeing himself from his bondage to a false sense of ego. In this respect it is more properly a psychology or even a psychotherapy than a religion.

The idea of God features very little in Buddhism. The Buddha himself is not worshipped or idolized; he is simply regarded as an example of a normal human being who, as a result of meditation and other practices, achieved enlightenment. He is venerated as a wise man, as a teacher and as a precept of enlightenment, but not as God.

Because of its strong emphasis on personal development, meditation techniques of one kind or another lie at the core of Buddhism. But because it has developed in many different directions with many different sects and approaches, there is no single meditation technique common to Buddhism in general. Instead there is a rich variety of techniques ranging from simple breathing exercises to the most laborious systems of ritual. Here we shall consider three of the principal schools: the Theravada Buddhism of Ceylon and South-East Asia, Tibetan Buddhism and Zen Buddhism, found in Japan and other Far Eastern countries.

Theravada Buddhism

Theravada is regarded as one of the most ancient schools of Buddhism. In the present day it is found mainly in Southern India, Ceylon, Burma, Thailand and other parts of South-East Asia. The most common form of Theravada meditation is called *Vipassana* which is best translated as 'insight'. As a complete beginner you would probably start by being asked simply to sit quietly and be aware of the breath. You would just be aware of the movement of the breath as the chest and diaphragm contract and expand. Sometimes you might be told to fix your attention on the navel and be aware of its movement with the rise and fall of the breath, and it is possibly this meditation that gave birth to the misguided idea of meditation being the concentration upon the navel.

As you sit meditating in this way, thoughts inevitably start rising in the mind – some enjoyable, some distracting and some even unpleasant. You are usually told simply to be open to whatever comes, to whatever emotion or sensation there may be in the body – just to accept it as it is, without forming an interpretation or a judgement.

Having started with awareness of some physical activity, the student may later progress to an awareness of feelings, sensations or thoughts. This passive, watchful approach is similar to that found in TM and many other techniques.

As you begin to develop the ability to be aware in a simple, innocent way, there may come a series of realizations concerning what is happening in the mind. It is at this stage, as you begin to understand the reasons for the flow of thoughts in the mind, that true 'insight' develops.

As you go deeper into meditation so the grip of old fantasies, old obsessions, old pictures which you have of yourself, your friends and the rest of the world begins to loosen. The aim is to become more aware of the thoughts which come and go in the mind, to become more conscious of what you are seeing, hearing and also to observe more closely your actions, and how and why you are doing them. If, for example, you suddenly found yourself becoming very angry, rather than venting this anger on another person, you may ask yourself where did this anger come from, exactly what is it you are angry about? Is it really something in the other person, or is it something in yourself? Maybe you are angry because somebody else has not lived up to your expectations, in which case it may be your expectations which are at fault rather than the other person. People usually find that once they have clearly defined the exact source of the anger, the anger itself dissolves.

It is generally held that those thoughts that arise during meditation come from past experiences which have not yet been finished with – the sort of unresolved situations which we would like to be able to forget but which keep on popping up. Simply by letting the thoughts come, without trying to suppress or analyse them, it is said that many of these past conflicts can begin to resolve themselves.

The ultimate goal, as with all forms of Buddhism, is the attainment of *nirvana,* the state of true enlightenment, the state in which one has become completely free from all conditioning by the past. Much of our time is spent projecting into the future, daydreaming, trying to predict what will happen, trying to make certain things happen or prevent other things from happening. Much of our time is also spent living in the past, analysing what went wrong or reliving those good experiences. Very seldom are we truly in the present, innocently being aware of what is happening in us and around us, free from any bondage to our past and future. In this respect *nirvana* may be thought of as becoming fully alive, living and enjoying each moment as it is, free from expectations, worries and desires.

Tibetan Buddhism

Tibetan Buddhism remained unknown to most people in the West until the Chinese invasion of Tibet in the 1950s, mainly as a result of the physical inaccessibility of the whole Tibetan plateau. Yet this physical isolation has protected the Tibetan schools of Buddhism from external influences and distortions, with the result that it is one of the strongest and most powerful schools, and has became the way of life for most of the Tibetan people.

When the Chinese invaded, some of the monks and lamas (a lama is roughly equivalent to an abbot) managed to escape across the border into Nepal and India, where they settled. Since then a few have come to the West, either on visits or to settle.

The principal Tibetan teachings in England have come from a group of three such lamas; Chime, Trungpa and Akong. After a short stay in Oxford, they settled near Dumfries, where they set up a small Tibetan centre, called Samye Ling. This was the first permanent centre in Britain for Tibetan Buddhism, and over the years it has attracted a great number of people from all walks of life. It is now run by just one of the three lamas, Akong. Trungpa went on to the United States to set up a number of centres there, while Chime moved down to East Anglia.

From Monday to Friday Chime is now a commuter. Like millions of other commuters he puts on his suit and tie, and, briefcase in hand, is driven by his wife to catch the train to London. By 9 o'clock he is by his desk in the British Museum where he catalogues Tibetan manuscripts. Apart from his Tibetan looks, Chime does not initially stand out, though a few regular commuters have begun to notice that he is always happy, very polite and has a delightful sense of humour. At week-ends he sheds his suit and tie, dons crimson and ochre robes and teaches meditation at the retreat centre near Saffron Walden. At both the centre in Scotland and this one in East Anglia people may stay for a week-end, a week, or longer to receive instruction in a variety of Tibetan Buddhist meditations.

As with most schools of Buddhism the Tibetans often use breathing techniques to help the mind settle down and become calm. Once this has been established you can then move on to more complex practices.

One of the most common types of meditation is the visualization of a Buddhist deity. Nearly all schools of meditation, both Buddhist and non-Buddhist, realize that the mind cannot just fall silent, and that initially there has to be some object of attention. In TM it is a mantra, and in *Vipassana* it is the breathing or feelings. In Tibetan techniques it is often the visualization of some deity.

Instead of trying to stop visual images floating into the mind, the process of visualization is built upon and the images are made even more powerful. A typical meditation would involve the visualization of a Buddhist deity, in full colour and with attention to the minutest detail. There may be other deities surrounding the chosen one, and possibly the image would also contain some syllables or mantras. At the same time you would recite a mantra connected with the deity, or maybe the most famous Buddhist mantra, *Om Mane Padme Om*, which might be translated as 'may the jewel of

the eternal lotus shine upon the world'.

This may all seem very complicated, and it may also sound like idol worship. But it is not really a form of worship. Each of the different deities has different qualities associated with it, and the aim of the meditation is to instil these qualities into your own life. Thus a headstrong, angry, short-tempered person who gets flustered rather quickly might be given a deity such as *Avalokiteshvara*, one of whose qualities is gentle compassion. Alternatively, a particularly self-effacing, meek and mild sort of person, who tended to sit in the background the whole time might be given the deity *Mahakala*, who looks like a ferocious demon, with blue skin, huge claws and fangs, and with flames pouring out of it. For many people this might sound a terrifying image to meditate upon, but for the meek and mild person it might be the very image which is needed.

The aim is to create a balance within the person by integrating both weak and strong aspects of the personality. As with most types of meditation the emphasis is not so much on the experience of meditation itself as on how meditation affects one's life.

Such visualization techniques are not always easy at first. We in the West do not use visualization to any great extent in our daily lives, and it may initially be difficult to hold on to an image in great detail. At first you may only get a very vague impression of the figure concerned, perhaps nothing but a patch of light. You start where you can, but with practice people usually find that they can learn to visualize quite complex images fairly easily.

Meditations such as these might take anything between ten and thirty minutes and, once learnt, can be easily done at home. There are, however, other Tibetan Buddhist techniques which take much longer, and often require you to go away on an extended retreat.

One such practice is the meditation known as the 'First Foundation'. This consists of one hundred thousand full-length prostrations. You start off standing up, holding the palms together in the traditional saintly position, silently repeating a mantra to yourself. At the same time you are probably maintaining a visual image of a deity, or perhaps of the lineage of Buddhist lamas from which the teaching has descended. You then kneel down; then lie down on your front, arms out-stretched, still repeating the mantra and visualizing the deity. Then you return to the kneeling position, and finally stand up again. That is one prostration, and it may take

opposite: Avalokiteshvara   45

anything up to a minute to do properly. The full meditation is to do one hundred thousand of them.

What is the value of such a technique for the average Westerner? Such practices may well seem something of a hang-over from another tradition and culture, and have little or no significance for us in the West. One of the justifications sometimes given is that the technique breaks the mind from the habit of going through the same old thought patterns time after time; if you make it do something else repeatedly you might possibly shake it out of its old habits. In this respect doing one hundred thousand prostrations is not essentially different from repeating a certain holy phrase to oneself a hundred thousand times. A second reason for doing it is to create a certain amount of humility, and for this it is obviously important that you approach the meditation with the correct attitude of mind.

Meditations such as these are not usually given to beginners. The lamas would only suggest their use where they judged it would be appropriate.

Another growing centre of Tibetan Buddhism in Britain is the Manjushri Institute, based in Cumbria at Conishead Priory. This centre is run by a different group of lamas who, until recently, have not taught much in the West. Like most Tibetan emigrés they have very small funds, but have been given enough money by various well-wishers to buy an old priory just south of the Lake District. Here, two or three Tibetan monks or lamas are always in residence, giving instruction to those who have come to live there and to others who are just visiting.

The priory itself is at present in a very poor structural condition. Most of the time the thirty or so residents are working on repairing the building, taking out the rotten beams, rebuilding fallen ceilings and so on. They estimate that it will probably take them ten years to complete the restoration.

Between the building operations they nevertheless do quite a bit of meditation, and instruction is usually given at least once a day. They also hold regular week-end courses to which people may go in order to get an introduction to some of the techniques taught there. They teach most of the Buddhist techniques already mentioned, and in addition place a lot of emphasis on chanting and the performance of Buddhist ceremonies.

Manjushri, after whom the centre is named, is a Buddhist deity, and many of the ceremonies are in her honour. Again this is not a form of worship or idolatry. One of Manjushri's qualities is compassion, and the rites are really directed to this quality of compassion that to any single being. The intended goal is to develop compassion within oneself; and not just compassion for other people, but for all beings everywhere.

Zen Buddhism

Early in its history Buddhism moved north and east, through Tibet into China and Japan, giving birth to what has become known as Zen Buddhism. Zen claims to be the essence of Buddhist teachings. It lays the greatest emphasis on personal instruction and the experience of enlightenment (that is, one's own buddha-nature) and heavily plays down all doctrines and scriptures. What teachings there are in Zen tend to be very terse and often paradoxical statements; phrases such as 'He who knows the Buddha, does not know the Buddha' and 'Before enlightenment chop wood and carry water, after enlightment chop wood and carry water'. Yet within such strange statements are often hidden very profound teachings, which the rational mind alone cannot grasp.

There are two principal schools of Buddhism, *Soto* Zen and *Rinzai* Zen. Both lay heavy emphasis on meditation, and both usually start with some form of breathing meditation similar to the *Vipassana* meditation, to help calm the mind down. The *Soto* sect goes on to the practice of *Zazen* meditation. This can be either a still, sitting meditation or an active, walking meditation.

In the still version you sit cross-legged, spine and head erect, hands folded one palm above the other, eyes open, being aware of the surroundings, attending to nothing in particular. The intention is that through this passive attitude of mind you eventually suspend logical analytical thinking, and with it all desires, attachments and judgements, leaving the mind in a state of relaxed attention. Unlike the other types of meditation we have been discussing so far, in *Zazen* you are not usually given a specific or thought process to attend to; the aim is to arrive directly at the state of still mind.

For most Westerners (and indeed for most Easterners), this can initially be a very difficult process. In Zen monasteries it is common for the *Roshi* (the abbot of the monastery) to watch the students carefully, and if he feels that anyone is losing attention or not sitting erect enough, to give them a thwack on the shoulders with a stick to restore their watchfulness.

In the active version of *Zazen*, the neutral attitude of neither despising nor cherishing the thoughts which arise in the mind is carried through into daily activity. So you may walk around, watching both your internal thought process and the world outside, trying to be in the present as much as possible. The ultimate aim is to be able to enter fully into any action while maintaining inner attention and clear awareness. This state corresponds to the state of enlightenment as described by most other schools of meditation, but in *Zazen* the aim is to go directly for the state itself. In some respects, therefore, it is the most direct form of meditation, but paradoxically it may also be the most difficult.

The other school of Zen, *Rinzai* Zen, uses meditation on paradoxical statements called *Koans*. These are puzzles which are insoluble by intellectual reasoning, and take the form of questions such as 'What was your face before you were born?' 'What is the sound of one hand clapping?' or 'What is Mu?'. The student meditates upon the *Koan* continuously, returning the mind to the problem whenever it wanders off. Periodically, maybe once a day, the *Roshi* will ask for the student's latest solution. Usually the solution has been arrived at through the normal thinking process, and the master consequently dismisses it.

By choosing an insoluble question the *Roshi* is trying to exhaust the rational intellectual mind. When finally the mind is totally frustrated and the student is at his wits' end, he may make the jump to *Satori*. The 'solution' becomes obvious, and at the same time he is said to see into his own true nature – the 'inside and outside merge into a single unity'. Essentially, the *Koan* has forced the student to transcend the linguistic modes of thinking which so dominate our mental activity and which usually prevent the mind from being still.

Although Buddhist techniques vary enormously from one school to another, there is very little dogmatism as to which way is 'correct'. And anyone who may by now be feeling a little confused by the plethora of different approaches may find solace in an alleged saying of the Buddha himself: 'Do not believe anything because you have read it in the scriptures, or because someone has told you; only when it accords with your own experience should you believe it.'

Buddhist centres in Britain

Information about most of the different types of Buddhism in Britain can be obtained from:

The Buddhist Society, 58, Eccleston Square, London SW1.
Telephone: 01–834 5858.

Vipassana. There are several organizations in Britain teaching this type of meditation. If you can get away for a few days the best place to start is:

The Vipassana Meditation Centre, Chapter House,
Gorefield Road, Leverington, Wisbech, Cambridgeshire.
Telephone: Wisbech 38383.

The emphasis here is very much on the teaching of meditation and its integration with a normal active life. There are none of the religious trappings which are found in some of the other centres. This centre also runs occasional retreats in other parts of Britain. Costs, as with most of the centres mentioned below, are modest, and cover basic accommodation. Details can be obtained by contacting the centres directly.

Tibetan Buddhism. The principal residential centres are:

Samye Ling Tibetan Centre, Eskdalemuir, Near Langholm, Dumfries and Galloway.
Telephone: Eskdalemuir 232

Kham Tibetan House, Rectory Lane, Ashdown,
Saffron Walden, Essex.
Telephone: Ashdown 415.

The Manjushri Institute, Conishead Priory, Ulverston, Cumbria.
Telephone: Ulverston 54019.

Zen Buddhism. Zen Buddhism requires a considerable amount of instruction from a teacher, and is probably not something a beginner could take up on his own. There are, however, several small Zen Buddhist communities in Britain where one can go and stay for a short period of time and receive the basic instruction. But be warned, they are usually quite strict. Details of these centres can be obtained from the Buddhist Society listed above.

The above list is by no means exhaustive. There are probably about fifty different Buddhist groups in Britain, and some of them teach meditation techniques not mentioned in this chapter. Again, the Buddhist Society will be of help to anyone wanting further details.

Further reading

DHIRAVAMSA, Vichitr Ratna *The way of non-attachment: the practice of insight meditation* Turnstone Press, 1975.

RAHULA, Walpola *What the Buddha taught* Gordon Fraser, 1967.

SUZUKI, D. T. *Essays in Zen Buddhism* 3 series. Rider, 1970.

THERA, Nyanaponika *The heart of Buddhist meditation* Rider, paperback 1969.

TRUNGPA, Chögyam *Meditation in action* Stuart and Watkins, 1969.

Devotional Meditation and Siddha Yoga

There exist many types of meditation in which devotion to the guru or to God play an important part. Most of these practices come from the Indian tradition called *Bhakti*, which has always seen devotion as an essential element. In this chapter we will look first of all at one practice, Siddha Yoga as taught by Baba Muktananda, examining some of the rationale and effects of this approach, and then briefly outline some of the different teachings and organizations.

Siddha Yoga

I have chosen Baba Muktananda because he gives a good insight into the thinking behind devotional practices, and also his own life has very much followed the traditional one of a *Bhakti*. He claims to have gained his own enlightenment through devotion to his Guru, Sri Nityananda. He spent many years in isolation in the middle of India, meditating in a hut, occasionally visiting his Guru for guidance, although he says he felt his master's presence continually.

He now runs a sizeable community – what in India is called an Ashram – at a place called Ganesh Puri. Most of his time there is spent looking after his growing number of students, although he does make the occasional visit to the West to give lectures and visit those who cannot go out to India.

The basic meditation he teaches consists of the repetition of the mantra *Om Namah Shivaya*, which roughly translated is 'I bow to Shiva'. In Hinduism, Shiva refers to one of the three principal deities. Although there are many different deities in Hinduism they are not separate gods, but are aspects of the one God (Brahman). In this respect, Shiva traditionally represents one of the three basic tendencies present in all creation. In this meditation, however, Shiva is seen as a symbol both of the Guru and one's own inner self.

The meditation is done as much as possible in groups, as this is said to enhance its effects. A typical session may start with half an hour's chanting from the '*Guru Gita*' ('*The Song to the Guru*'), a long Sanskrit devotional text. This is then followed by the repetition of the mantra. Some of this may be chanted aloud to music, and some of it is done silently within. While repeating the mantra you may also be reflecting on its significance and meaning, as this also is said to enhance the meditation.

One of the basic teachings of Baba Muktananda is that the

opposite: Baba Muktananda

essence of the Guru is also the essence of your own self. Surrender and devotion to the Guru (symbolized as Shiva) is seen as a way of surrender and devotion to one's own inner nature. Your devotion to the Guru is therefore a tool to help you release some of your own innate potential.

One of the goals of this meditation is the receiving of *Shaktipat*. *Shakti* is the name given to an inner, psychic energy which everyone is said to possess, although for most of us it may be repressed or locked up, and *Shaktipat* means the descent of that energy. It is equivalent to what other Indian traditions know as the raising of *Kundalini*. This energy, which is often symbolized by a serpent, reflects the feminine aspect of the universe. In its dormant state it is said to rest at the base of the spine. When, through meditation and devotion, the energy is awoken and begins to rise up the spine, she enlivens other 'nerves' and centres in the body and, on reaching the crown of the head (what is called the thousand-petal lotus), she unites with consciousness, the masculine aspect of the universe. From this union a sublime nectar is said to flow down in blissful waves throughout the body.

These centres, and the nerves radiating from them, do not generally correspond to the nerves and nerve centres known to Western physiology. But this does not mean that the Hindu model is totally invalid. It is not so much a physical model of the body as a psychic model. It serves to relate some of the inner experiences which come through meditation with sensations which may be felt in different parts of the body.

In Siddha Yoga the *Shaktipat* can be received in many different ways. Some may 'receive' it merely as a result of being in the presence of the Guru. Some from simply hearing of the Guru, or even from seeing his photograph. Some receive it through meditation and use of the mantra. For some people it may come through a dream – very often a dream of the Guru, or some symbolic wise man. For others it may come not through any contact with the Guru, but by simply opening oneself to one's self.

The experiences which follow receiving the *Shaktipat* can be equally varied. You may hear the sound of bells or music; you may see lights of various colours and sizes; you may feel the body shaking; the breathing may quicken and become very rapid; or you may feel intense waves of blissful energy flowing through the body.

Many of these experiences probably happen in the other meditation techniques we have been looking at, but whereas most teachers tend not to emphasize them, lest the student become too concerned with gaining the experience rather than with the process of meditation, Baba Muktananda uses these experiences as signposts on the path. In his book *The Play of consciousness*, he discusses in considerable depth the nature of many of these experiences, and the significance of the sounds and lights which may be seen during meditation. There is, however, the danger that if a person beomes too concerned with such experiences, he may start imagining them to be happening or otherwise unconsciously delude himself that certain states of meditation are taking place.

The general effects claimed for Siddha Yoga are the same as with most other meditation techniques. It seems to result in a decrease in stress and tension, and an increase in general calmness and serenity. People claim that they become much more stable as a result of the practices and often that they change their whole outlook on life, losing some of the desperate need for 'keeping up with the Joneses'. This does not mean that followers of Baba Muktananda renounce the material world: most of them tend to be ordinary family people with regular jobs and otherwise normal life styles. The difference is that they become less attached to the material world.

As with the students of Bhagwan Rajneesh, those who get more deeply into this way of meditation often take on new names, though they do not in this case change their clothes as well. The reasons given for this change are similar – to lessen one's identity with the past, and to have a name which is related to one's own personal qualities and attributes.

The difficulty with any devotional path is that you have to await the awakening, and very often it comes through chance, or the grace of God, rather than through your own efforts. Most spiritual teachers proclaim that the greatest force in the universe is the force of love, and that the highest path is therefore the path of love, ultimately the love of God. If the Guru is a manifestation of God in a physical body, the way to love God is to love the Guru. This is all very well if you have been fortunate enough to have the kind of experience which leads you to see the Guru as God, or any other experience which directly opens your heart to him. But if the Guru is merely another teacher, the love is not flowing in the first place, and again there is the danger of creating a false mood of devotion and surrender.

As a general conclusion, therefore, we might again refer to the teachings of the Buddha. If a technique does work for you then that is absolutely fine; if it does not, there are still plenty of other things to try.

Centres. Baba Muktananda does not attract a large following in Britain at the moment. Compared to Maharishi's Transcendental Meditation, it is very small indeed. There are a number of groups in Britain which meet regularly for meditation. Details can be obtained from:

Muktananda Meditation Centre, 1, Bonneville Gardens, London SW4.
Telephone: 01–673 0877.

Further reading

MUKTANANDA, Paramahansa *The play of consciousness* Berkeley, Calif: SYDA Foundation, 1974; Harper and Row, paperback 1979.

There are in Britain a number of other devotional groups, all generally small though taken together their following probably amounts to between five and ten thousand. Below are some of the principal groups:

Sri Chinmoy

Sri Chinmoy was born in India and spent the first half of his life there studying meditation. He later moved to America, and now lives in New York, where he is among other things an adviser to the United Nations on meditation and spiritual affairs. One of his principal teachings is 'love, devotion and surrender'. In meditation this is practised using Sri Chinmoy as an object of love, devotion and surrender. He is himself renowned for a very powerful 'presence', and his devotees claim just sitting in a room with him can have a remarkably stilling and even enlightening effect upon the mind. Some non-devotees who have met him have also reported similar effects.

London Centre:
c/o 16d, Portland Road, London W11.
Telephone: 01—727 9680.

The Divine Light Mission

The Divine Light Mission is an organization set up by the Guru Maharaji Ji when he was a young boy. His devotees tend to live together in small communities, believing that it is important to be surrounded by other people who are following a similar path in life. Meditation consists partly of devotion to the Guru, and also of withdrawing the senses in order to become aware of inner sounds and inner lights.

London Centre:
Divine Light Mission,
131, Clapham High Street, London SW4.
Telephone: 01–622 9261.

Meher Baba

Meher Baba was a spiritual teacher living in India in the first half of the century, who, because of his extraordinary claims and rather unusual life style, attracted considerable interest from Western seekers. From 1925 onwards he stopped speaking to anyone, continuing to communicate only by the use of a simple alphabet board, pointing out the letters and words in rapid succession. This complete silence was maintained for over forty years until he died in January 1969. One of the puzzles about Meher Baba was that he always claimed that he would one day break his silence and utter the word which would 'shake the universe'. He died, however, without breaking his silence. Throughout his teaching Meher Baba also claimed to be the *Avatar* – that is to say, a manifestation of God. In India it is often claimed that God manifests from time to time as some such avatar, though Christians may find this a very difficult idea to accept. Again, as with other devotional practices, you probably first need to feel a genuine love for the master if the devotion is to be successful.

London Centre:
Meher Baba Centre, 3a, Eccleston Square, London SW1.
Telephone: 01–834 4212.

Radha Soami Satsang

This group has descended from the Sikh tradition rather than the Hindu tradition, and devotees follow the inspiration of their Sikh leader, Charan Singh. They are a small but very serious group who lead fairly strict life styles, avoiding meat, alcohol, cigarettes, and generally emphasizing 'a clean and upright life'. They tend to get up very early in the morning, often around 6 o'clock, in order to fit in as much as two hours' meditation before the day begins. Charan Singh himself claims that his teaching is very close to that of Christ and sees no conflict whatsoever between his path and the Christian path. This organization does not advertise its presence, but keeps very quiet, believing that anyone who is seriously interested in obtaining information will find them when they are ready.

Contact:
Sant Mat, c/o National Westminster Bank,
34, Henrietta Street, London WC2.

Christian Meditation

Meditation has always existed within the Christian tradition, although in recent history it has not usually been given the same emphasis as in Hinduism and Buddhism. The Eastern religions have been more concerned with raising the consciousness of the individual and have seen meditation as one of the prime ways of achieving this. Christianity, on the other hand, has become more concerned with worship, prayer and the leading of a Christian life. Meditation as such has been mainly confined to the inner circles of the Church – to priests, monks, nuns and others deeply committed to the Church. As far as the general public is concerned, meditation has receded into the background. In recent years, however, the growing general interest in meditation has led some clergy to bring the practice back and to start teaching it to their congregations, as is the case at All Saints Church, Isleworth.

The meditations taught within the Christian tradition can conveniently be divided into two groups; discursive meditation and non-discursive meditation.

Discursive meditation might be described as thoughtful meditation. Its most common form is a reflection on a quotation from the Bible, or upon some other spiritual passage, and the aim is to come to a greater insight and understanding of the message behind the word. Thus you might meditate upon St Paul's phrase, 'I live; yet not I, but Christ liveth in me', or upon Christ's parable of the sower, and you would ponder at length upon the different levels of meaning. In everyday speech we might talk of this as contemplation, but within the Christian tradition the term contemplation actually refers to the other principal type of meditation, non-discursive meditation.

There are several different types of non-discursive meditation practised by Christians, but what they all have in common is that they do not involve the logical rational mind. They are not concerned with reaching intellectual insights so much as with bringing the mind to that state of quiet which is the goal of most other meditative techniques.

One meditation is simply to sit in silence, to sit in the presence of God. This is the type of meditation described by the monk Brother Lawrence in his book *The practice of the Presence of God*. He worked in a monastery kitchen and his meditation was to try to maintain an uninterrupted mental silence and alertness, holding the mind to an inner stillness as he carried out his duty in the kitchen.

This is the 'direct' approach, and as such is somewhat similar to the active Zazen of Zen Buddhism.

Some Christian techniques concentrate the awareness upon the breathing in much the same way as do some of the Theravada Buddhist techniques. Another type of Christian meditation uses visualization. In the Christian tradition you may direct your attention on to the visual symbol of the crucifix, or upon more complex images such as the Madonna and Child, an icon or some other picture. As with the Tibetan practices of visualization, one of the purposes of this meditation is to enliven some of the qualities of the image, usually qualities of compassion, within yourself. Another type of visualization technique sometimes practised by Christians is simply to imagine yourself surrounded by white light, being washed over by the light and becoming one with it.

One of the best-known Christian meditations, and one which dates back to the very early days of Christianity is the Jesus Prayer. In its most popular form this consists of the silent inward repetition of the phrase 'Lord Jesus Christ, Son of God, have mercy on me, a sinner'. The aim is to keep repeating this phrase to yourself throughout meditation, and in some cases throughout the day as well. The phrase may sometimes by shortened to 'Jesus Christ, have mercy on me' or even simply to 'Jesus'.

This last form of the meditation is often known as the Prayer of Simplicity, both on account of the simplicity of the phrase involved, and on account of the simplicity of the technique. The word 'Jesus', or 'Father' or 'God' or whatever else is used may be thought of as the Christian equivalent of a mantra, and is generally used in much the same way as in Eastern techniques, the attention just floating along gently on the phrase concerned, with no effort or concentration.

This type of meditation is most common in the Eastern Orthodox Church, particularly the Russian Orthodox Church, where it has always been practised both in the monastic tradition and by the lay people. Here it is often known as the Prayer of the Heart. While silently repeating the word 'Jesus' or, in its original form, the short phrase 'Kyrie eleison' you hold the attention to your heart – not so much the physical heart as the centre of the chest, which is often taken to be the emotional centre of the human being.

It is interesting that there are close parallels between Christian techniques such as the Prayer of Simplicity and the Prayer of the

Heart, and Transcendental Meditation and some of the Buddhist meditations we looked at earlier. Indeed, some of the descriptions by mediaeval Russian monks of the Prayer of the Heart are almost exactly the same as the instructions given to people today when they learn Transcendental Meditation. In both cases you are instructed to think the sound or mantra quietly to yourself, not concentrating on it but just letting the process flow by itself. When intruding thoughts enter the mind, the meditator does not bother about them, but simply returns the attention to the word concerned. Exactly the same attitude is found in Theravada Buddhism, only in this case the mantra has been replaced by the gentle rising and falling of the breath. It would appear that the same basic technique has been employed many times throughout history and in many different cultures, and one is led to the conclusion that it must therefore be a very natural and effective method of stilling the mind.

There are of course differences between the Prayer of the Heart and techniques such as Transcendental Meditation, differences which probably reflect the different attitudes of the cultures concerned. These subtle differences probably also account for the slightly different effects of the techniques. In Transcendental Meditation, for example, the mantra has no meaning as far as the meditator is concerned (though it may have meaning in the original Sanskrit). In Christian meditation the meaning of the phrase chosen is very important. Meditation is often seen as a calling upon 'Jesus' or 'The Father', and although the meditator may not be dwelling on the meaning, it is obviously important that the right word be used.

Another difference between Christian meditation and TM is that the attitude of TM is very secular. It is mainly concerned with teaching meditation to the man in the street, getting him to relax and also to begin to expand his awareness. Consequently, most of the effort is put into making sure that the technique is learned and practised correctly. With Christian meditation, on the other hand, the meditator must usually be deeply committed to the Church. Here faith is very important – not blind faith, but the feeling of inner security which comes from the experience of meditation coupled with belief that he or she is cared for and loved by God. Such a faith is deepened by meditation, and at the same time can lead to deeper states of meditation. It not only brings a greater sense of inner security but can also become the basis of a great compassion towards other people. This again is a common aim of most meditative techniques.

In Christianity meditation is closely linked to prayer. Prayer is commonly thought of as some form of petition or request to God, usually done on one's knees in a beseeching position. But this is only the most superficial form of prayer. In its deepest sense true prayer comes from a feeling of oneness with God. In this state there are no words, no talking, just a direct communion from a state of inner silence. Meditation, therefore, by bringing about this state of inner silence, can be seen as a valuable aid to a state of true prayer. Moreover, scriptures both Christian and non-Christian testify to the fact that when a person's consciousness is in this state of stillness then whatever is desired is fulfilled. Thus we can see how our everyday sense of prayer could have descended from this deeper sense of inner prayer.

Various techniques of meditation are slowly being reintroduced by the Church to the general public. In Coventry Cathedral and St Albans Abbey, for example, special meditational Eucharists held once a month in which the sacraments of bread and wine are given in the context of meditation. The congregation is completely silent. They are encouraged to relax both their bodies and their minds, and to quieten the flow of thoughts coming up from within. Once the mind has become still they usually practise a short form of the Prayer of Simplicity, and perhaps some exercise of visualization, imagining themselves being bathed in the love and light of God. From this state of inner quiet the congregation is led straight into the Prayer of Thanksgiving and the consecration of the bread and wine.

A completely different approach to the reintroduction of meditation into the Church is taken at St Mary Woolnoth situated in the City of London, right in the heart of the banking area. Here simple relaxation exercises are being introduced into the Church, during the lunch-time break. Secretaries, executives, office staff and managers gather in the church and are led through a series of progressive relaxation exercises. The aim is partly to help these people to cope with the stress of city life, but also to get them more in touch with their own bodies and their own feelings.

Many people come along to the sessions rather apprehensive that they are being 'conned' into a religious service. They are usually rather relieved to find they do not have to say prayers or join in hymns. The intent is that through the relaxation exercises they realize that they can be a little more in touch with God, and feel a little more love and compassion towards others, without actually having to put it all into words. Quite a lot of people find this a very useful first step towards deeper meditation and true prayer.

Further information on Christian meditation and retreats can be obtained from:

Association for Promoting Retreats, Church House, Newton Road, London W2 5LS
Telephone: 01–727 7924.

Secretary of the Open Centres, Avils Farm, Lower Stanton, Chippenham, Wiltshire
Telephone: Seagry 720202.

The Guild Church of St Mary Woolnoth, Lombard Street, London EC3.
Telephone: 01–626 9701.
(Informal lunch-time classes, Wednesdays 1.15–1.45 p.m.)

Rev. Peter Dewey, All Saints Church, Church St., Isleworth, Middlesex TW7 6BE
Telephone: 01–568 4645.

The Roman Catholic National Retreat Council, Damascus House, Mill Hill, London NW7.
Telephone: 01–959 8971.

Father Matthew, Grâce-Dieu, Fox Lane, Boars Hill, Oxford, OX1 5DN

Further reading

ABHISHIKTANANDA *Prayer* SPCK, 1972.
BLOOM, Anthony *Living prayer* Darton, Longman and Todd, 1966.
HAPPOLD, F.C. *Prayer and meditation* Penguin Books, 1972. (Currently out of print but available in many public libraries).
ISRAEL, Martin *An approach to mysticism* Churches' Fellowship for Psychical and Spiritual Studies, 1968.
KHARITON, Igumen of Valamo *The art of prayer* translated by E. Kadloubovsky and E. M. Palmer. Faber, 1966.
TUGWELL, Simon *Did you receive the spirit?* Darton, Longman and Todd, 1975.
VERNEY, Stephen *Into the new age* Fontana, 1976.
The way of a pilgrim translated by R. M. French. SPCK, 1972.